To Eric,

With Metta
from the Valley Sangha.

Wherever you go ....
Like This

RUMI

Like This

VERSIONS BY
Coleman Barks

For this *moment*

Cover: "Dervishes" by Ingrid Schaar

RUMI: *Like This*
Copyright © 1990 Coleman Barks
All rights reserved.

Library of Congress Catalog Card Number 89-092393
ISBN 0-9618916-2-9

Contents

	Introduction — "Love and Silence"	7
	These Versions of Rumi	9
1823	"I don't get tired of you. Don't grow weary . . . ."	11
3079	"We've come again to that knee of seacoast . . . ."	12
3090	"Forget the world, and so . . . ."	13
2922	"Candle, wine and Friends, ..."	14
2061	"Give yourself a kiss."	15
1888	"There is some kiss we want . . . ."	16
2039	"Go to your pillow and sleep, my son."	17
314	"Those who don't feel this Love . . . ."	18
393	"Stay together, Friends."	19
1373	"I was dead, then alive."	20
1022	"Yesterday at dawn, my Friend said, *How long* . . . ."	22
1826	"If anyone asks you . . . ."	23
2627	"You are the King's son."	25
824	"Whose idea was this, ..."	26
1052	"There's a tradition that God can be seen . . . ."	27
1001	"What was in that candle's light . . . ."	28
1047	"When it's cold and raining, ..."	29
3050	"The Lord of Beauty enters the soul . . . ."	30
1957	"An intellectual is all the time showing off."	31
2266	"Circulate the cup and take me out of . . . ."	32
2625	"Science and theology would be just whims . . . ."	33
2577	"There is a Community of the Spirit."	35
1620	"There is a passion in me . . . ."	37
532	"Advice doesn't help Lovers!"	38
2707	"Where are those who died serving God . . . ."	40
1126	"Don't unstring the bow."	41
1837	"I wish I knew what You wanted."	42
2083	"If my words are not saying what You . . . ."	43
2006	"Jasmine comes up where You step."	44
2155	"How does a part of the world leave . . . ."	45

2357   "You are granite."   47

110   "Don't worry about saving these songs!"   48

543   "When I press my hand to my chest, ..."   49

940   "Love has taken away my practices . . . ."   51

1615   "I may be clapping my hands, ..."   53

1195   "You that love Lovers, ..."   54

1590   "There is a Sun-star rising . . . ."   55

1397   "Of these two thousand 'I' and 'We' people, ..."   56

1910   "Notice how each particle moves."   57

1092   "This is the Night of Union, ..."   58

1304   "No more wine for me!"   59

911   "On the day I die, when I'm being . . . ."   56

171   "When I see Your face, the stones . . . ."   62

Notes   63

Love and Silence

We know very little of Shams of Tabriz, the elusive Master who wandered the Near East in the 13th Century, seeking ever higher levels of mystical companionship. The legend is that one night he cried out from his longing, "Lord, show me one of Your Beloved Ones!"

A Voice came, "What will you give in exchange?"

"My head."

"The hidden Truth you search for is Jelaluddin Rumi."

So it seems an agreement was struck in the invisible world, and in late October of 1244, in Konya, Turkey, they met. Their subsequent Friendship is one of the Mysteries. With them, the categories of Teacher and student, lover and Beloved, Master and disciple, dissolved. They entered into the months-long periods of solitude and deep communion called *sohbet*. But some in the community were disturbed by this Friendship. Several times Shams was forced into exile, though always he returned at Rumi's request. Then, one night in May of 1247, while they were on retreat, Shams was gently called from outside.

He knew it was to his death. "I am called to the torture."

Rumi waited a long while to answer. "There is only One whose right it is to call. Answer That."

The Aflaki account, which I am following here, tells then that as the ambushers struck, Shams cried out, *There is no Reality but God* with such force that the conspirators fell to the ground unconscious. When they came to, there was no trace of Shams except for a few drops of blood.

After Shams' disappearance, Rumi broke into the spontaneous river of his poetry, more and more of which is gradually being brought over into English. Over a thousand of his odes end with some reference to Shams. In fact, he called the entire collection of his odes and quatrains the *Divani Shamsi Tabriz,* the *Works of Shams of Tabriz.* Rumi closes more than five hundred other odes with reference to *khamush,* the Persian word for Silence. Those two endings are the double-noted theme in this collection.

There is a powerful stage of spiritual growth where longing for the Friend, the Beloved, is a consuming passion, a burning. And there is another place where that personal longing for God gets pushed over into a vast Silence. These poems come from both places. Or is it one place, the verge of fire and wordlessness?

Every "form" of the Beloved gets taken away. We love some person, or place, or condition, and then the wineglass breaks, and we "fall toward the Glassblower's Breath." In the *like this* refrain poem (p.23) Rumi says that we eventually *become* what the poetic likenesses point to, and see the world from the other side of longing. We become the breathing Divine Presence *(Hu)*, and Shams Himself looks out through our eyes.

The "You" here makes personal the connection with the inspired spring these words overflow from, Shams of Tabriz being the primary pulse of that. But "Shams" means "the sun," and the *You* pronoun opens out into existence, everything the sun lights! Love for the Friend, the Beloved, the Kingdom Within, (in Persian, *kibriya,* the Grandeur, *asmat,* the Majesty), these are some of the terms for what's celebrated here, though there can be no definitive synonym. There are no words, and "any image is a lie." Silence is a deeper way that Lovers have found.

These poems are spontaneous unfoldings into a current, and like the best love poems of any tradition they melt into their being drawn, even as they keep a fierce reserve.

Meher Baba once made this connection between love and a profound quietness:

> When a person is angry with another person, that person is removed from his heart. That's why the physical reaction is to shout. The greater the distance, the louder the shouting. But when individuals are in love, they speak softly, and when they are still further in love, no words are needed.

An intensity seals the lips. When water begins to boil, the cook puts a lid on the pot. Rumi's Silence is that of the chef, who hands you a spoon to let you taste, now that the recipe-reading is over. The Silence becomes an inward communion, an experience beyond any doctrinal description.

References

Aflaki, Ahmad ibn Mohammad, *Manaqeb al-arefin,* Agra, 1897; Ankara, 1959–60, 2 vols., Turkish translation, Ankara, 1964. French translation by Clement Huart, *Les Saints des Dervishes Tourneurs,* Paris, 1918–20. Excerpts from that are collected, in English, in a little booklet called *The Whirling Ecstasy* distributed by Sufi Islamia, 65 Norwich St., San Francisco, CA 94110.

Anzar, Naosherwan, ed. *The Ancient One: A Disciple's Memoirs of Meher Baba,* The Meher Baba Work, P.O. Box 10, New York, N.Y. 10188. Meher Baba's words here are as quoted by Eruch Jessawala. Meher Baba himself was silent from July 10, 1925 until his death in 1969. He did, however, use an alphabet board and a unique system of hand gestures to give discourses. Those have been collected in a single volume: *Discourses,* available from Sheriar Press, 3005 Highway 17 North Bypass, Myrtle Beach, S.C. 29577.

These Versions of Rumi

In January of 1977 the linguist John Moyne (Head of Linguistics, CUNY) and I began our collaborative effort of translating the poetry of Jelaluddin Rumi. For twelve years John has been sending me literal translations of the poems from Persian, and I have worked with those to make what I hope are valid poems in English. (*Open Secret* [1984], *Unseen Rain* [1986], and *This Longing* [1988] have been published by Threshold Books; *We Are Three* [1987] by Maypop Books; *These Branching Moments* [1988] by Copper Beech.) When John, busy with other projects, cannot translate fresh materials, I often turn to the scholarly renderings of Arberry. (A. J. Arberry, *Mystical Poems of Rumi.* Persian Heritage Series No. 3. Chicago: The University of Chicago Press, 1968. A. J. Arberry, *Mystical Poems of Rumi.* Persian Heritage Series No. 23. Boulder, Colorado: Westview Press, 1979.) This collection comes from that work.

Coleman Barks
December 8, 1989

1823

I don't get tired of You. Don't grow weary
of being compassionate toward me!

All this thirst-equipment
must surely be *tired* of me,
the waterjar, the water-carrier.

I have a thirsty fish in me
that can never find enough
of what it's thirsty for!

Show me the way to the Ocean!
Break these half-measures,
these small containers.

All this fantasy
and grief.

Let my house be drowned in the wave
that rose last night out of the courtyard
hidden in the center of my chest.

Joseph fell like the moon into my well.
The harvest I expected was washed away.
But no matter.

A fire has risen above my tombstone hat.
I don't want learning, or dignity,
or respectability.

I want this music and this dawn
and the warmth of your cheek against mine.

The grief-armies assemble,
but I'm not going with them.

This is how it always is
when I finish a poem.

A Great Silence overcomes me,
and I wonder why I ever thought
to use language.

We've come again to that knee of seacoast
no ocean can reach.

Tie together all human intellects.
They won't stretch to here.

The sky bares its neck so beautifully,
but gets no kiss. Only a taste.

This is the food that everyone wants,
wandering the wilderness, "Please give us
Your manna and quail."

We're here again with the Beloved.
This air, a shout. These meadowsounds,
an astonishing myth.

We've come into the Presence of the One
who was never apart from us.

When the waterbag is filling, you know
the Water-carrier's here!

The bag leans lovingly against Your shoulder.
"Without You I have no knowledge,
no way to touch anyone."

When someone chews sugarcane,
he's wanting this Sweetness.

Inside this globe the soul roars like thunder.
And now Silence, my strict tutor.

I won't try to talk about Shams.
Language cannot touch that Presence.

Forget the world, and so
command the world.

Be a lamp, or a lifeboat, or a ladder.
Help someone's soul heal.
Walk out of your house like a shepherd.

Stay in the spiritual fire.
Let it cook you.

Be a well-baked loaf
and lord of the table.

Come and be served
to your brothers.

You have been a source of pain.
Now you'll be the delight.

You have been an unsafe house.
Now you'll be the One
who sees into the Invisible.

I said this, and a Voice came to my ear,
"If you become this, you will be *That!*"

Then Silence,
and now more Silence.

A mouth is not for talking.
A mouth is for tasting this Sweetness.

Candle, wine, and Friends,
on a Springlike night
in mid-December.

This love I have for You
makes everywhere I look
blaze up. The tip
of every feather burns.

A deep Sweetness comes through sugarcane,
into the cut reed,
and now it's in the empty notes
of the flute.

Beheaded Lovers don't complain.
They live hidden underground,
like people in lava cities.

There is no worse torture than knowing *intellectually*
about Love and the Way.

Those Egyptian women,
when they saw Joseph, were not *judging*
his handsomeness.

They were lost in it,
cutting their hands
as they cut their food.

Muhammed was completely empty
when he rose that Night
through a hundred thousand years.

Let wind blow through us.
Let Shams cover
our shadows
like snow.

Give yourself a kiss.
If you live in China, don't look
somewhere else, in Tibet, or Mongolia.

If you want to hold the beautiful one,
hold yourself to yourself.

When you kiss the Beloved,
touch your own lips with your own fingers.

The beauty of every woman and every man
is your own beauty.

The confusion of your hair
obscures that sometimes.

An artist comes to paint you
and stands with his mouth open.

Your love reveals your beauty,
but *all* coverings would disappear
if only for a moment your holding-back
would sit before your generosity
and ask,
   "Sir, who *are* You?"
        At that,
Shams' life-changing face
gives you a wink.

There is some kiss we want
with our whole lives,
the touch of Spirit on the body.

Seawater begs the pearl
to break its shell.

And the lily, how passionately
it needs some wild Darling!

At night, I open the window
and ask the moon to come
and press its face against mine.
Breathe into me.

Close the language-door,
and open the love-window.

The moon won't use the door,
only the window.

2039

Go to your pillow and sleep, my son.

Leave me alone in the passion
of this death-night.

Let the mill turn with your grieving.
But stay clear. Don't fall
into the river with me.

There's no way out,
no cure but death.

Last night in a dream I saw an old man
standing in a garden.

It was all Love.
He held out his hand and said,
Come toward me.

If there is a dragon on this path,
that old man has the emerald face
that can deflect it.

This is enough.
I am leaving my self.

Bahauddin, my son,
if you want to be impressively learned,
memorize a famous historian,
and quote him as someone else!

314

Those who don't feel this Love
pulling them like a river,
those who don't drink dawn
like a cup of springwater
or take in sunset like supper,
those who don't want to change,

let them sleep.

This Love is beyond the study of theology,
that old trickery and hypocrisy.
If you want to improve your mind that way,

sleep on.

I've given up on my brain.
I've torn the cloth to shreds
and thrown it away.

If you're not completely naked,
wrap your beautiful robe of words
around you,

and sleep.

Stay together, Friends.
Don't scatter and sleep.

Our Friendship is made
of being awake.

The waterwheel accepts water
and turns and gives it away,
weeping.

That way it stays in the garden,
whereas another roundness rolls
through a dry riverbed looking
for what it thinks it wants.

Stay here, quivering with each moment
like a drop of mercury.

I was dead, then alive.
Weeping, then laughing.

The power of Love came into me,
and I became fierce like a lion,
then tender like the evening star.

He said, "You're not mad enough.
You don't belong in this house."

I went wild and had to be tied up.
He said, "Still not wild enough
to stay with us!"

I broke through another layer
into joyfulness.

He said, "It's not enough."
I died.

He said, "You're a clever little man,
full of fantasy and doubting."

I plucked out my feathers and became a fool.
He said, "Now you're the candle
for this assembly."

But I'm no candle. Look!
I'm scattered smoke.

He said, "You are the Sheikh, the Guide."
But I'm not a Teacher. I have no power.

He said, "You already have wings.
I cannot give you wings."

But I wanted *His* wings.
I felt like some flightless chicken.

Then New Events said to me,
"Don't move. A sublime generosity
is coming toward you."

And Old Love said, "Stay with me."

I said, "I will."

You are the fountain of the sun's light.
I am a willow shadow on the ground.
You make my raggedness silky.

The soul at dawn is like darkened water
that slowly begins to say *Thank you, thank you.*

Then at sunset, again, Venus gradually
changes into the moon and then the whole nightsky.

This comes of smiling back
at Your smile.

The Chess Master says nothing,
other than moving the silent chess piece.

That I am part of the ploys
of this game makes me
amazingly happy.

Yesterday at dawn, my Friend said, *How long
will this unconsciousness go on?*

*You fill yourself with the sharp pain of Love,
rather than its fulfillment.*

I said, "But I can't get to You!
You are the whole dark night,
and I am a single candle.

My life is upsidedown
because of You!"

The Friend replied, *I am your deepest being.
Quit talking about wanting Me!*

I said, "Then what is this
restlessness?"

The Friend, *Does a drop
stay still in the Ocean?*

*Move with the Entirety,
and with the tiniest particular.*

*Be the moisture in an oyster
that helps to form one pearl.*

If anyone asks you
how the perfect satisfaction
of all our sexual wanting
will look, lift your face
and say,

> *Like this.*

When someone mentions the gracefulness
of the nightsky, climb up on the roof
and dance and say,

> *Like this?*

If anyone wants to know what "spirit" is,
or what "God's fragrance" means,
lean your head toward him or her.
Keep your face there close.

> *Like this.*

When someone quotes the old poetic image
about clouds gradually uncovering the moon,
slowly loosen knot by knot the strings
of your robe.

> *Like this?*

If anyone wonders how Jesus raised the dead,
don't try to explain the miracle.
Kiss me on the lips.

> *Like this. Like this.*

When someone asks what it means
to "die for love," point

> *here.*

If someone asks how tall I am, frown
and measure with your fingers the space
between the creases on your forehead.

> *This tall.*

The soul sometimes leaves the body, then returns.
When someone doesn't believe that,
walk back into my house.
Like this.

When lovers moan,
they're telling our story.
Like this.

I am a sky where spirits live.
Stare into this deepening blue,
while the breeze says a secret.
Like this.

When someone asks what there is to do,
light the candle in his hand.
Like this.

How did Joseph's scent come to Jacob?
Huuuu.

How did Jacob's sight return?
Huuuuu.

A little wind cleans the eyes.
Like this.

When Shams comes back from Tabriz,
he'll put just his head around the edge
of the door to surprise us.
Like this.

You are the King's son.
Why do you close yourself up?
Become a Lover.

Don't aspire to be a General
or a Minister of State.

One is a boredom for you,
the other a disgrace.

You've been a picture on a bathhouse wall
long enough. No one recognizes you here, do they?

God's Lion disguised as a human being!
I saw that and put down the book
I was studying, Hariri's *Maqamat*.

There is no early and late for us.
The only way to measure a Lover
is by the grandeur of the Beloved.

Judge a moth by the beauty of its Candle.

Shams is invisible because He is inside sight.
He is the intelligent Essence
of what is everywhere at once, seeing.

Whose idea was this,
to have the lover visible
and the Beloved *in*visible!

So many people have died of their desiring
because of this. The lover cannot kiss
the lips he wants, so he bites himself!

Satisfaction is always two bow-shots away,
and yet something in the soul
prefers this unreachable Lover
to anyone reachable.

This being locked-in,
is better than having the keys
to any consolation-house.

The Beloved's rejection is wanted more
than anyone else's acceptance.

World-happiness is nothing.
Look for what Bestami had, for what
Sanai and Attar wrote of.

A beautiful meal looks delicious.
Then one night passes, and the food passes
through you, becoming repellent filth.

Eat love-food.
Suckle the toes of a Lion,
as the baby Abraham did in the cave.

But you should put away what you learned
as a foetus in your cave, that need for blood.

There is a tall tower that Love builds.
Live there in Silence.

The One who knows all secrets
is here *now,* nearer
than your jugular vein.

There's a tradition that God can be seen
in the color red. In the lights
that come from red hair!

They draw you, don't they?
The Unknowable Spirit has eyebrows
and eyes and skin!

Muhammed in a living form!
He looked at people!

Hundreds of doors swung open.
Then His form went away,

and this *praising sound*
flooded the world.

What was in that candle's light
that opened and consumed me so quickly?

Come back, my Friend! The form of our love
is not a created form.

Nothing can help me but that Beauty.
There was a dawn I remember

when my soul heard something
from Your soul. I drank water

from Your Spring and felt
the current take me.

1047

When it's cold and raining,
You are more beautiful.

And the snow brings me
even closer to Your Lips.

The Inner Secret, that which was never born,
You are That Freshness, and I am with You now.

I can't explain the goings,
or the comings. You enter suddenly,

and I am nowhere again.
Inside the Majesty.

The Lord of Beauty enters the soul
as a man walks into an orchard
in Spring.
          Come into me
that way again!
             Light the lamp
in the eye of Joseph. Cure Jacob's
sadness. Though you never left,
come and sit down here and ask,
"Why are you so confused?"

Like a fresh idea in an artist's mind,
you fashion things before they come into being.

You sweep the floor like the man
who keeps the doorway.
             When you brush
a form clean, it becomes
what it truly is.

You guard Your Silence perfectly
like a waterbag that doesn't leak.

You live where Shams lives,
because your heart-donkey was strong enough
to take you there.

An intellectual is all the time showing off.
Lovers dissolve and become bewildered.

Intellectuals try not to drown,
while the whole purpose of love
is drowning.
                    Intellectuals invent
ways to rest, and then lie down
in those beds.
                    Lovers feel ashamed
of comforting ideas.
                    You've seen a glob
of oil on water? That's how a lover
sits with intellectuals, there, but alone
in a circle of himself.
                    Some intellectual
tries to give sound advice to a lover.
All he hears back is, *I love you.*
I love you.
                    Love is musk. Don't deny it
when you smell the scent!
                    Love is a tree.
Lovers, the shade of the long branches.

To the intellectual mind, a child must learn
to grow up and be adult.
                    In the station of love,
you see old men getting younger and younger.

Shams chose to live low in the roots
for you. So now, he soars in the air
as your sublimely articulating love!

Circulate the cup and take me out of
who I am and what I've done,
my name and my shame.

You Who Pour the wine, keep after me.
Trick me! When I have none of Your joy,
I worry about everything. Lay your traps.

I should fast. Someone who fasts
visits the Friend at night.

But often I come in the front door,
and You fly through the roof!
Be more patient!

Muslims, what is there to do?
I'm burning up and yet unsatisfied.

There's no cure but the taste
of what the saints pass around.

The story of Lovers has no end,
so we'll be happy with this,
just this, *Goodbye*.

And the answer to Mutanabbi's riddle is,
"Someone whom *no* wine consoles."

Science and theology would be just whims of the wind,
if you knew full surrender.

These beautiful world-birds would seem like flies,
if that wing-shadow fell across you.

The famous drums would sound like tapping sticks.
If that dawn rose, you'd be released
from whatever is holding you.

What you thought was ahead
would be behind.

One word, one *letter,* from that book,
and you'd understand.

Your fire wavers in the thought of death,
but if it burned with Eternity,
it would not tremble.

Those you are traveling with
keep you distracted.

Open your mouth to this wind,
and let a straw catch in your throat.

Choke and die
of the worthlessness
you value.

Your childish intelligence got stuck
at "He frowned," that part of the *Qur'an*
where Muhammed's revelations are interrupted
by a wandering blind man.

Muhammed frowns, then turns
to the man's true intention.

After frowning, comes "Blessed is He."
Reach through your worrying to That.

This Silence. This Moment.
Every *moment,*

if it's genuinely inside you,
brings what you need.

There is a community of the Spirit.
Join it, and feel the delight
of walking in the noisy steeet,
and *being* the noise.

Drink *all* your passion,
and be a disgrace.

Close both eyes
to see with the Other Eye.

Open your hands,
if you want to be held.

Consider what you've been doing!
Why do you stay with such a mean-spirited
and dangerous partner?

For the security of having food, admit it!
Here's a better arrangement: Give up this life,
and get a hundred new lives.

Sit down in this circle.

Quit acting like a wolf, and feel
the Shepherd's Love filling you.

At night, your Beloved wanders.
Don't take pain-killers.

Tonight, no consolations.
And don't eat.

Close your mouth against food.
Taste the Lover's mouth in yours.

You moan, "But she left me. He left me."
Twenty more will come.

Be empty of worrying.
Think of Who Created Thought!

Why do you stay in prison
when the door is so wide open?

Move outside the tangle of fear-thinking.
Live in Silence.

Flow down and down in always
widening rings of Being.

There is a passion in me
that doesn't long for anything
from another human being.

I was given something else,
a cap to wear in both worlds.
It fell off. No matter.

One morning I went to a place beyond dawn.
A source of sweetness that flows
and is never less.

I have been shown a beauty
that would confuse both worlds,
but I won't cause that uproar.

I am nothing but a head
set on the ground
as a gift for Shams.

Advice doesn't help Lovers!
They're not the kind of mountain stream
you can build a dam across.

An intellectual doesn't know
what the drunk is feeling!

Don't try to figure
what those lost inside love
will do next!

Someone in charge would give up all his power,
if he caught one whiff of the wine-musk
from the room where the Lovers
are doing who-knows-what!

One of them tries to dig a hole through a mountain.
One flees from academic honors.
One laughs at famous mustaches!

Life freezes if it doesn't get a taste
of this almond cake.
                    The stars come up spinning
every night, bewildered in love.
                            They'd grow tired
with that revolving, if they weren't.
                            They'd say,
"How long do we have to *do* this!"

God picks up the reed-flute world and blows.
Each note is a need coming through one of us,
a passion, a longing-pain.
                        Remember the Lips
where the wind-breath originated,
and let your note be clear.
Don't try to end it.
Be your note.
                    I'll show you how it's enough.

Go up on the roof at night
in this city of the Soul.

Let *everyone* climb on their roofs
and sing their notes!

Sing loud!

Where are those who died serving God
on the plain of Karbala?

                Where are those who know how
to open the gate? There's no rational answer
to this. A prison full of debtors
has been let out!

              Where has everyone gone?
Where are *you!*

            You're in the Ocean
of which this world is just the foam
thrown up on shore.

                Something huge inside me surges,
and the *foam* of this poetry takes *form*.

Let foam-form be.

             Dive into the burning Ocean
      as that Source of Light, Shams,
comes up in the East.

Don't unstring the bow.
I am Your four-feathered arrow
that has not been used yet.

I am a strong knife-blade word,
not some *if,* or *maybe,*
dissolving in air.

I am sunlight slicing the dark.
Who made this night?
A forge deep in the earth-mud.

What is the body?
Endurance.

What is love?
Gratitude.

What is hidden
in our chests?
Laughter.

What else?
Compassion.

Let the Beloved be a hat pulled down firmly on my head.
Or drawstrings pulled and tied around my chest.

Someone asks, How does love have hands and feet?
Love is the sprouting-bed for hands and feet!

Your father and mother were playing love-games.
They came together, and you appeared!

Don't ask what Love can make or do!
Look at the colors of the world.

The riverwater moving in all the rivers at once.
The truth that lives in Shams' face.

I wish I knew what You wanted.
You block the road and won't give me rest.
You pull my lead-rope one way, then the other.
You act cold, my Darling!
Do You hear what I say?

Will this night of talking ever end?
Why am I still embarrassed and timid about You?
You are thousands. You are One.
Quiet, but most articulate.

Your Name is Spring.
Your Name is Wine.
Your Name is the nausea
that comes from wine!

You are my doubting
and the lightpoints
in my eyes.

You are every image, and yet
I'm homesick for You.

Can I get there?
Where the deer pounces on the lion,
where the One I'm after's
after me?

This drum and these words keep pounding!
Let them both smash through their coverings
into Silence.

2083

If my words are not saying what You would say,
slap my face. Discipline me as a loving mother does
a babbling child caught up in nonsense.

A thirsty man runs into the sea, and the sea
holds a sword to his throat.

A lily looks at a bank of roses
and wilts and says nothing.

I am a tambourine. Don't put me aside
till the fast-dancing starts.
Play me some all along.
Help me with these little sounds.

Joseph is most beautiful when he's completely naked,
but his shirt gives you an idea,
as the body lets you glimpse the glitter
on the water of the soul.

Even if the corpse-washer binds my jaw shut,
you'll still hear this song
coming out of my dead-silence.

Jasmine comes up where You step.
You breathe on dirt, and it sails off
like a kite. You wash Your hands,
and the water You throw out shines with gold.

You say the first line of the *Qur'an,*
and all the dead commentators lift their heads.

Your robe brushes a thornbush,
and a deep chord of music comes.

Whatever You break finds itself more intelligent
for being broken. Every second a new being
stands in the courtyard of Your chest
like Adam, without a father or a mother,
but the beginning of many generations to come.

I should rhyme that fifty times!

The beginning of many
generations to come,

a line without any
inclination to end!

But I won't. I close my mouth
in hopes You'll open Yours.

How does a part of the world leave the world?
How can wetness leave water?

Don't try to put out a fire
by throwing on more fire!
Don't wash a wound with blood!

No matter how fast you run,
your shadow more than keeps up.
Sometimes, it's in front!

Only full, overhead sun
diminishes your shadow.

But that shadow has been serving you!
What hurts you, blesses you.
Darkness is your candle.
Your boundaries are your quest.

I can explain this, but it would break
the glass cover on your heart,
and there's no fixing that.

You must have shadow and light-source both.
Listen, and lay your head under the Tree of Awe.

When from that tree, feathers and wings sprout
on you, be quieter than a dove.
Don't open your mouth for even a *cooooooo*.

When a frog slips into the water, the snake
cannot get it. Then the frog climbs back out
and croaks, and the snake moves toward him again.

Even if the frog learned to hiss, still the snake
would hear through the hiss the information
he needed, the frog-voice underneath.

But if the frog could be completely silent,
then the snake would go back to sleeping,
and the frog could reach the barley.

The soul lives there in the silent Breath.

And that grain of barley is such that,
when you put it in the ground,
it grows.
      Are these enough words,
or shall I squeeze more juice from this?

Who am I, my Friend?

You are granite.
I am an empty wine glass.

You know what happens when we touch!
You laugh like the sun coming up laughs
at a star that disappears into it.

Love opens my chest, and thought
returns to its confines.

Patience and rational considerations leave.
Only passion stays, whimpering and feverish.

Some men fall down in the road like dregs thrown out.
Then, totally reckless, the next morning

they gallop out with new purposes. Love
is the Reality, and poetry is the drum

that calls us to that. Don't keep complaining
about loneliness! Let the fear-language of that theme

crack open and float away. Let the priest come down
from his tower, and not go back up!

Don't worry about saving these songs!
And if one of our instruments breaks,
it doesn't matter.

We have fallen into the place
where everything is music.

The strumming and the flute notes
rise into the atmosphere,
and even if the whole world's harp
should burn up, there will still be
hidden instruments playing.

So the candle flickers and goes out.
We have a piece of flint, and a spark.

This singing-art is sea foam.
The graceful movements come from a pearl
somewhere on the ocean floor.

Poems reach up like the edge of driftwood
along the beach, wanting and wanting!

They derive
from a slow and powerful root
that we can't see.

Stop the words now.
Open the window in the center of your chest,
and let the spirits fly in and out.

When I press my hand to my chest,
it is Your Chest.

And now You're scratching my head!

Sometimes you put me in the herd
with Your other camels.

Sometimes You place me at the front of the troops
as the commander. Sometimes You wet me
with Your mouth like You do Your seal-ring
just before You plant Your power.

Sometimes You round me
into a simple door-knocker.

You take blood and make sperm.
You take sperm and create an animal.
You use the animal to evolve Intelligence.
Life keeps leading to more Life.

You drive me away gently
as a flute-song does a dove
from the eaves.

With the same song
You call me back.

You push me out on many journeys;
then You anchor me with no motion at all.

I am water. I am the thorn
that catches someone's clothing.

I don't care about marvelous sights!
I only want to be in Your Presence.

There's nothing to *believe*.
Only when I quit believing in myself
did I come into This Beauty.

I saw Your Blade and burned my shield!
I flew on six hundred pairs of wings like Gabriel.
But now that I'm Here, what do I need wings for?

Day and night I guarded the pearl of my soul.
Now in this Ocean of pearling currents,
I've lost track of which was mine.

There is no way to describe You.
Say the end of this so strongly
that I will ride up over
my own commotion.

Love has taken away my practices
and filled me with poetry.

I tried to keep quietly repeating,
No strength but Yours,
but I couldn't.

I had to clap and sing.
I used to be respectable and chaste and stable,
but who can stand in this strong wind
and remember those things?

A mountain keeps an echo deep inside itself.
That's how I hold your Voice.

I am scrap wood thrown in your Fire,
and quickly reduced to smoke.

I saw You and became empty.
This Emptiness, more beautiful than existence,
it obliterates existence, and yet when It comes,
existence thrives and creates more existence!

The sky is blue. The world is a blind man
squatting on the road.

But whoever sees Your Emptiness
sees beyond blue and beyond the blind man.

A great soul hides like Muhammed, or Jesus,
moving through a crowd in a city
where no one knows Him.

To praise is to praise
how one surrenders
to the Emptiness.

To praise the sun is to praise your own eyes.
Praise, the Ocean. What we say, a little ship.

So the sea-journey goes on, and who knows where!
Just to be held by the Ocean is the best luck
we could have. It's a total waking-up!

Why should we grieve that we've been sleeping?
It doesn't matter how long we've been unconscious.

We're groggy, but let the guilt go.
Feel the motions of tenderness
around you, the buoyancy.

1615

I may be clapping my hands,
but I don't belong to a crowd of clappers.
I'm neither this nor that.

I'm not part of a group that loves flute music,
or one that loves gambling,
or one that loves drinking wine.

Those who live in time, descended from Adam,
made of earth and water, I'm not part of that.

Don't listen to what I say,
as though these words came from an inside
and went to an outside.

Your faces are very beautiful,
but they are wooden cages.

You'd better run from me.
My words are fire.

I have nothing to do with being famous,
or making grand judgments,
or feeling full of shame.

I borrow nothing.
I don't want anything from anybody.

I flow through all human beings.
Love is my only companion.

When Union happens, my speech goes inward,
toward Shams. At that meeting,

all the secrets of language
will no longer be secret.

1195

You that love Lovers,
this is your home. Welcome!

In the midst of making form, Love
made this form that melts form,
with love for the door, and
Soul, the vestibule.

Watch the dust grains moving
in the light near the window.

Their dance is our dance.

We rarely hear the inward music,
but we're all dancing to it nevertheless,

directed by Shams,
the pure joy of the sun,
our Music Master.

There is a Sun-star rising
outside the reality of form.

I am lost in that other Reality.
It's sweet not to look at two worlds,
to melt in meaning as sugar melts in water.

No one tires of following the soul.
I don't recall now what happens
on the manifest plane.

I stroll with those I have always wanted to know.
Fresh and graceful as a waterlily, or a rose.

The body is a boat, and I am waves
swaying against it.

Whenever it anchors somewhere,
I smash it loose, or smash it to pieces.

If I get lazy and cold, flames come
from my Ocean and surround me.

I laugh inside them like gold,
purifying myself.

A certain song makes the snake
put his head down on a line in the dirt. . . .
Here is my head, brother.
What next!

Weary of form, I came into Qualities.
Each Quality says, "I am a blue-green sea.
Dive into me!"

I am Alexander at the outermost extension
of empire, turning all my armies inward,
toward the meaning of armies, and Shams.

Of these two thousand "I" and "We" people,
which am I?

Don't try to keep me from asking!
Listen, when I'm this out of control!
But don't put anything breakable in my way!

There is an Original inside me.
What's here is a mirror for that, for You.

If You are joyful, I am.
If You grieve, or if You're bitter, or graceful,
I take on those qualities.

Like the shadow of a cypress tree in the meadow,
like the *shadow* of a rose, I live
close to the Rose.

If I separated my self from You,
I would turn entirely thorn.

Every second, I drink another cup of my own blood-wine.
Every instant, I break an empty cup against your door.

I reach out, wanting You to tear me open.

Saladin's generosity lights a candle in my chest.
Who *am* I then?
His empty begging bowl.

Notice how each particle moves.
Notice how everyone has just arrived here
            from a journey.
Notice how each wants a different food.
Notice how the stars vanish as the sun comes up,
            and how all streams stream toward the ocean.

Look at the chefs preparing special plates
            for everyone, according to what they need.
Look at this cup that can hold the Ocean.
Look at those who see the Face.
Look through Shams' eyes
            into the Water that is
            entirely jewels.

This is the Night of Union,
when the stars scatter their rice
over us. The sky is excited!

Venus cannot stop singing the little songs
she's making up, like a bird
in the first warm Spring weather.

The North star can't quit looking over
at Leo. Pisces is stirring milky dust
from the Ocean floor. Jupiter
rides his horse over to Saturn, "Old Man,
jump up behind me! The juice is coming back!
Think of something happy to shout as we go."

Mars washes his bloody sword, and puts it up,
and begins building things. The Aquarian water jar
fills, and the Virgin pours it generously.

The Pleiades and Libra and Aries
have no trembling in them anymore.

Scorpio walks out looking for a lover,
and so does Sagittarius!

This is not crooked walking, like the Crab.
This is the Holiday we've been waiting for.

It's finally time
to sacrifice Taurus
and learn how the sky
is a lens to look through.

Listen to What's Inside
anything I say.

Shams will appear at dawn,
and then even this night will change
from its Beloved Darkness
to a Day beyond any ordinary,
sweet daylight.

No more wine for me!
I'm past delighting in the thick red
and the clear white.

I'm thirsty for my own blood
as it moves into a field of action.

Draw the keenest blade you have
and strike, until the head circles
about the body.

Make a mountain of skulls like that.
Split me apart.

Don't stop at the mouth!
Don't listen to anything I say.
I must enter the center of the fire.

Fire is my child,
but I must be consumed
and become fire.

Why is there crackling and smoke?
Because the firewood and the flames
are still talking:
                    "You are too dense. Go away!"
"You are too wavering. I have solid form."

In the blackness those two friends keep arguing.
Like a wanderer with no face.
Like the most powerful bird in existence
sitting on its perch, refusing to move.

What can I say to someone so curled up with wanting,
so constricted in his love?

Break your pitcher against a rock.
We don't need any longer
to haul pieces of the Ocean around.

We must drown, away from heroism,
and descriptions of heroism.

Like a pure spirit lying down, pulling
its body over it, like a bride her husband
for a cover to keep her warm.

On the day I die, when I'm being
carried toward the grave, don't weep.

Don't say, "He's gone! He's gone!"
Death has nothing to do with going away.

The sun sets and the moon sets,
but they're not *gone*. Death
is a coming together.

The tomb *looks* like a prison,
but it's really release
into Union.

The human seed goes down in the ground
like a bucket into the well where Joseph is.

It grows and comes up full
of some unimagined beauty.

Your mouth closes here
and immediately opens
with a shout of joy there.

When I see Your Face, the stones start spinning!
You appear; all studying wanders.
I lose my place.

Water turns pearly.
Fire dies down and doesn't destroy.

In Your Presence I don't want what I thought
I wanted, those three little hanging lamps.

Inside Your Face the ancient manuscripts
seem like rusty mirrors.

You breathe; new shapes appear,
and the music of a Desire as widespread
as Spring begins to move
like a great wagon.
                    Drive slowly.
Some of us walking alongside
are lame!

Notes

2039 (p. 17) — The deathbed poem. Aflaki, a contemporary of Rumi's grandson, comments that this seems to be Rumi's last poem, spoken to his son Bahauddin (Sultan Veled), comforting him, sending him off to get some sleep, and ending with the calling-after, the wonderful lighthearted jibe at his son's intellectual pretensions!

2266 (p. 32) — Mutanabbi's riddle. Mutanabbi is the famous panegyrist who wrote in Arabic (915-965). There are many puzzles about him, much discussion of plagiarism in his poetry. In his youth he was actually imprisoned for leading an insurrection in al-Samawa, in which he set himself up as a prophet with a new *Qur'an*. "Mutanabbi" means "the man who pretended to be a prophet." I have not been able to locate the Mutanabbi riddle to which Rumi gives the answer here. Perhaps it was "Who is the Friend?" Or "Who pours this Wine?"

Rumi Books and Tapes
Available from Maypop

Open Secret (Threshold, 1984) — 83 pp. A selection of odes, quatrains, and selections from the *Mathnawi*, with Introduction. Winner of a Pushcart Writers' Choice Award. $8.00.

Unseen Rain (Threshold, 1986) — 83 pp. One hundred and fifty short poems from Rumi's *Rubaiyat,* with Introduction. $8.00.

We Are Three (Maypop, 1987) — 87 pp. Odes, quatrains, and sections of the *Mathnawi.* With notes. $7.50.

These Branching Moments (Copper Beech, 1988) — 52 pp. Forty odes, with Introduction. $6.95.

This Longing (Threshold, 1988) — 107 pp. Sections from the *Mathnawi,* and Letters, with Introductions. $9.00.

Delicious Laughter (Maypop, 1990) — 128 pp. Rambunctious teaching stories and other more lyric sections from the *Mathnawi,* with Introduction. $7.50.

Like This (Maypop, 1990) — 68 pp. Forty-three odes, with Introduction. $7.50.

Open Secret & **Unseen Rain** set — Two volumes, hardbound, black linen with gold lettering. $18.00.

Open Secret audio cassette (1987) — Various selections read by Dorothy Fadiman and Coleman Barks, with musical accompaniment. $9.95.

Poems of Rumi, a two-cassette package (2½ hrs). Poems read by Robert Bly and Coleman Barks, with various musical accompaniments. $15.95.

New Dimensions Radio Interview (1986) — Coleman Barks discusses Rumi with interviewer Michael Thoms (1 hr.). $7.00.

Postage and Handling: all items: $1.00 for the first, and 25¢ for each additional item. Order from: MAYPOP BOOKS, 196 Westview Drive, Athens, GA 30606. Telephone (404) 543-2148.